day residue

POEMS & PROSE BY

WANDA DEGLANE

Day Residue

Cover image by Wanda Deglane

Printed in the United States of America

ISBN-13: 9798715071132

https://wandadeglane.wixsite.com/poetry

ALSO BY WANDA DEGLANE

Rainlily (2018)

Things that Will Happen After the End of the World No One Will Be Around to Witness (post ghost press, 2018)

Lady Saturn (Rhythm & Bones Press, 2019)

Honey-Laced Garbage Dreams (Ghost City Press, 2019)

Bittersweet (Vegetarian Alcoholic Press, 2019)

Missed Connection (Rinky Dink Press, 2019)

passionfruit (2020)

Venus in Bloom (Porkbelly Press, 2020)

penumbra (Ghost City Press, 2020)

PULP (Maverick Duck Press, 2020)

MELANCHOLIA (Vegetarian Alcoholic Press, 2021)

DAY RESIDUE

CONTENTS

"In what I think is a dream,
I look at some manifestation of the past
& say, *I know you're not real.*"

-Maggie Smith, *Joke* (2018)

The following pieces are based on dreams I've had, ten years ago or last night or any time in between. While some pieces may comprise multiple dreams mashed together, none of them are made up.

BLOOD MOON

when you are nine years old, you dream you're walking your dog with your mom and brother down a seemingly endless sidewalk. it's barely six o'clock but the moon is out, so huge it chokes out half the horizon. your mother is saying, *we have to hurry, the blood moon is coming.* you want to ask her what she means, but she's running now. *hurry, hurry!* you're chasing her, legs moving like molasses. red starts to spread across the moon, like drops of blood across a toilet bowl, two thousand miles wide. your mother is screaming, smothered out by a roaring cackle. birds and rabbits scatter in all directions. you're not going to make it. your body drops to the pavement, quick and hard and unforgiving.

GARDEN LUNGS

your lungs have gone missing and you're not sure how— one minute, you were writing words in a journal you now know will be undecipherable, the next, you're gasping for air that refuses to stay in your body. you stumble into the kitchen, clutching your chest, and your mother scowls at you, exasperated, says, *really? you lost them again? well, you better go find them.* you swallow every plant you can find— daisies and peace lilies and weeping figs and mother-in-law's tongue— until your cavities fill with oxygen, sweet and singing. you venture all over town, searching behind honeysuckles and dilapidated bus benches, hanging up signs that read, *HAVE YOU SEEN THESE LUNGS? pink and squishy, left is longer than right. call with any information. URGENT. PLEASE HURRY.* days pass with no news, no sightings. your body begins to feel more like a garden than a burning bridge. the days melt into weeks. you bleed nectar now, your skin tastes honey-sweet when you bruise. hummingbirds and bumblebees make a home out of your hair, your ears only know the sound of deafening buzz and tiny wings beating thunder. you wake one morning and run to the bathroom to cough up hydrangea petals, soft rainbow spewing out of your throat. you look into the mirror to see your face tinged pale green— your flesh now feels waxy, little leaves bud from your arms. rushing out into your backyard, you scream into the flame-stained sky. you try to say, *where are you?* but your tongue is forgetting what it was like to once be animal. and then you hear it, the mewling, squeaky and faint. you tear apart walls and shrubs to finally find kittens in a hole dug under your house, weeks old and curled up in a familiar raw organ. your lungs balloon to their full capacity to house all six wriggling bodies, the just-opened baby eyes look up at you as if pleading. in your heart you know they need the lungs more than you do. you walk home as the sun climbs her way up, feeling the hush of new things growing in your body, wondering how long you have left before they absorb you completely.

DRIVE DRIVE DRIVE

more often than flying, you dream of / driving
all over the city, past the skyscrapered fingers /
of downtown Phoenix / and fields of copper roses / the
stereo is surely broken / as it only plays / a soft
ringing, with / an occasional hushed voice / whispering
sonnets / and the clinking of a teaspoon / it takes
several miles before you realize / you've never learned
how to drive before / panic sets in, wild and shivering
so hard / your sleeping body rattles / the road becomes /
pitted and twisting / like your spine / you brake so hard,
your heart / stops several yards farther than the rest of you /
breathing hard, you check yourself in the mirror / short,
silvery blonde hair meets / your gaze / where long
brown waves had once been / you do not recognize
these fingers / these freckles / numb, you start the car /
what do you do when you're surely not you? / nothing,
you decide, and speed down the interstate / as
the clouds eat the stars / you drive deep / into the
morning's arms without blinking / as if you've been
doing this for decades / you don't have a destination /
in mind, but the longer you drive / the more your hands
morph / into ones you know / your hair grows darker /
your eyes lighter / you pass buildings made of sky / and
bare-boned cities / and gas stations overtaken by ivy /
that sell songbirds instead of fuel / you're not sure
how many moons have passed / when you decide to
pull over / you reach a tumbledown motel / its neon sign
winking at you from miles away / standing outside are
three women / dressed in powder blue smocks / as you
approach them, they smile wide / with sharpened ruby
knives for teeth / and eyes black as buttons / you tear

your eyes away at once / and drive faster / *this is the only way I learn how to drive* / you think to yourself / *when I'm running from something* / *from everything* / late in the afternoon, you pass a large, colorful sign / that screams / *WELCOME TO A LOVELESS LAND* /

close your eyes / step on the gas.

GOOD BOY

you dream it's five years from now. you're picking your little sister up from school, walking her down the dark hallway where the older kids used to make out in the shadows. your childhood dog is walking into the nurse's clinic, his sun-drenched fur gleaming. you could have sworn he died so long ago, you still have his ashes in your living room. but you see him now and it's all gone: the fog in his eyes, the melon-sized tumors, the shrieks and creaks of his bones. you ask your sister what's going on, and she says, *didn't you hear? he replaced the old school nurse when she retired.* you call out his name but he doesn't seem to hear. he struggles to open the door with his paws, but makes it inside, and you run after him, peering into his clinic through the window. inside are children of all shapes and ages, seated and wailing. some have limbs missing, or wounds pit their skin like a hailstorm. others' skulls are caved in, black-red blood oozing from the fissures, others' flesh are at various stages of decay. you're physically ill, a scream is crashing around in your throat. your dog finally sees you, his eyes cloud-soft, his mouth stretching into his droopy, sweet smile.

TOOTH DECAY

you dream all the time / of
losing your teeth. you know / it's
not a very uncommon dream,
but / you can't help feeling / the rush
of panic / as you google its meaning.

the night you hide / in the bathtub
with your dog as a little girl / and you
turn on the roaring water / to drown
out the sounds of your parents' / screaming,
the thumps / the unraveling, you dream later /
that your newly born / front teeth fall out
without a fight / you run screaming / to your
mother, but when / she turns, her face is /
a smooth, blank, wicked mound.

on the day your / high school
boyfriend leans in / and whispers,
you know you deserve this / you make me /
have to love you this way / and you can't
stop the tremors / all the way home /
you dream the teeth / rot black in your
mouth / they wobble and fall / one by one /
on the left side of your face / where
a bruise now flowers.

and one day the man you called
friend / reaches beneath your skirt /
when he thinks / no one watches / and
though your knees / smack together,
you stumble over the words / to make him

stop / so he doesn't / and so you're
running / to the dentist / barefoot down
a crumbling street / trying to shove the
teeth / back into your gums / but you choke
on them in your haste / and the road goes
on for all eternity / and the teeth keep falling.

every time you wake / you lie petrified in
the dark / count each tooth with your tongue /
finally let out / the breath you were holding /
when not a single tooth wiggles / and collapse
with relief.

the last time / you spoke to your mother,
you dream / all your teeth / fall out /
in an instant / every last one / and since
you have no one left to run to / you crawl
under your bed to hide / from the bloodshot sky /
and the air that tastes of / rusted metal / you slide
your tongue across / your bare, puckered gums /
and weep / the next morning, you're afraid
to count / but find each tooth still there / solid
as walls.

you've stopped feeling relieved long ago.

GUILLOTINE OF SUNLIGHT

you're building a house at sunset
the sky is on fire   but it's still too dark
to see your bloody hands.   you can't stop.
you can't stop.
you tell the nurse
you only keep these bruises   as souvenirs
you never did like needles anyway.   so she smiles
sweet   like a wasp
and gives you a bigger bruise
to remember her by.   you're turning into
an offbeat mosaic of
sickly yellows and purples   and greens.
you're finally becoming   a masterpiece.
you see a girl   at the end of the road
and chase her for hours under
august's first   gloomy humidity, only to find
she was the sun the whole time
and now you're on fire.
you're building a house at sunset
but all your hammers were swallowed
by the steaming cesspool sky,
and now the void is asking you
to take back your screams.
in this movie you're watching,   doctors prepare
for emergency   heart surgery,
only to open the man up
and find his body   stuffed full of lettuce and
shredded
mozzarella cheese.   (you're holding
his real heart in your hands, in a jar   filled with tree sap
and frostbitten fingers.

this is a horror movie.)   now a family is stumbling
half-dead   through a desert,
skinned by broken-glass winds.   you've never seen
such raw redness before.
you want to look away but
you can't stop.
gnarled hands are reaching   for your limbs
like tree branches,   your phone is blasting
a song you haven't heard in ages,
a forgotten love,
you're pressing every button   but the music won't stop.
you're smashing your phone against
the pavement,
slice your fingers on   its cruel pieces
but the song plays on.
you're building a house at sunset,
choked by a haboob that turns the heavens
the color of disintegrating wine.   rain is falling upwards,
water sucked into the sky—   nothing wails louder
than melting ice,
than the planet dancing its own   death march.
you're building a house at sunset, but   no one
will ever live here, and   twin moons
already absorb the earth in their giant lady-mouths.
a man you don't recognize is   grabbing you
by the shoulders, he's screaming
in your face,   *can you still feel god?*

BATH OF TEARS

you're lying in a bathtub in the middle of a wasteland. there is nothing here but trembling silence and drunken stars that wink down at you and sizzle your skin. you fill the tub with your tears, but with no one to watch you, you forget to feel embarrassed. you think of all the people who hurt you, the ones who looked you in the eye with a scorching knife-gaze and said *I hope you don't mind how much I've taken from you. how much I'll keep taking.* you mourn how you used to be able to cry so freely and speak so loudly and walk in the darkness without fear of what's surely hunting you. you think up a version of yourself that is able to stand up and say *FUCK YOU FUCK YOU.* you wish you had her mouth. the stars are expanding, exploding, devouring you in light. this bath of tears is up to your chin. you're calling everyone you know and screaming *I don't need you anymore.* no one picks up. your signal is dying just like those stars. you keep dialing screaming dialing screaming dialing

WHAT DOES IT MEAN

this time, you know you're dreaming, but you're fashioning
a weapon out of anything you can find in this
stranger's bathroom anyway. shampoo bottles.
flower-laden soaps. a frayed loofah. something massive
is throwing itself into the door, slams thunder
the entire house and you know should it make its way
inside, it would obliterate you. you're grabbing fistfuls
of your hair, screaming *what does it mean what does it mean*
and the booms suddenly go quiet. everything inside
your body is quaking. the air is still for so long,
the silence births even bigger silences. from outside,
you hear a shudder. a croaking sound like stopped breath. the little
whine of a child. you dig your nails into the tile
as the door is ripped from its hinges, bit by bit
like a tree pulled from the earth by its roots

RECURRING NIGHTMARES

your living room floor is covered in cats.
your father steps on them, uncaring, little
spines snapping with each stomp. you are in
a tiny crawl space, black tar up to your shins.
something is whispering. you're trying to
masturbate but, one by one, every person
on earth interrupts you. you die horny and
bored. everyone you know is trying to kill you,
and you can't remember how to fly away. it's
the end of the semester and you've completely
forgotten about a class you signed up for. your
parents call you a disappointment. the man
who once throttled you now follows you
wherever you go, watching wordless and
omnipotent like an ugly god. you remember
how to fly but immediately plummet into
the ocean. you beat your little sister to death.
her one remaining eye blank, wet. *wait, stop*,
you're crying. *I've been here before. stop. stop,*
but the man keeps kissing you anyway, giddy
and faceless. your mother is holding you,
smoothing your hair, spoon-feeding rat poison
into your open mouth. *I love you*, she says.
I love you so much, it hurts.

IN ONE SLEEP

you're melting through planets / air cradling your body until it takes on / new shapes / and when galaxies collide it sounds like a quiet, sleepy sigh / a woman has stopped screaming / you don't remember when she started / a man tells you she's run out of oxygen / you take her out of his pocket and only / mangled body parts come loose / intestines coiling around your torso / you're vomiting feathers, the man tells you / to look closer / those body parts are octopus tentacles / and each one wiggles so lightly / like they're waving at fireflies / each sucker is a pearl and they lodge their pearls in your head / you say *I know everything now* / it occurs to you that everything you own lived a decent life before you / that your brother always knew you are gay / that all your heroes are frightened / and it occurs to you that you're dreaming / you say, *there are two parts of me / one of me is in this body, in this moment / the other is sleeping / and we are two vastly different people* / the man leans close / says, *there's a third part of you as well / and that one's the most important / who is she?* you ask / and he stabs you in the kneecaps / and you forget at once about / dreaming / and the three you's / *why did you do that,* you say / and he explains, *if you want the world to love you / then we must also break your kneecaps* / you ponder this very deeply / gaze down at the handles of knives now coming out of your knees / the trails of blood spiraling to your feet / and an old friend is taking your hand now / and he's saying, *look* / you're on a beach, a small island / *this is where I came from* / your friend is waving his arms, breathless and happy / *my whole family, this is our home* / he's spilling tears / and his tears become lilies, dotting the shore / *we know it so well / every grain of sand / every leaf on every tree / every flame that swallowed the land / when death fell howling from the sky* / you say, *I'm sorry, what* / and it's fifteen years later / and you're trying to go upstairs but the stairs are gone / you don't mind springing from one floor to the other / but it's starting to rain / billions of gallons pouring from red-eyed clouds / a canopy of scales caves in on itself / each scale shrieks and hisses and finally falls quiet / your twin daughters are shielding themselves from the downpour / *run inside,* you tell them / *it's been raining all day / it's barely noon,* one daughter says / and you glance around you, blinking hard / glass is shattering in your brain / *happy birthday, mom* / says your daughter, and you're nodding along / *that's right* / the skin on your hand wrinkles, then flattens again / *there's something I have to show you,* you tell your daughters / *but it was upstairs, and the stairs are gone / what do you mean?* your partner is beside you now / *they're right there* / and sure enough the stairs are in front of you / cascading down hundreds of stories / the man from before is right below you, and he's charging up / the man from before is your father / and you recognize the death-cold murder in his eyes / you're stumbling back / no one is going to save you this time / your father is on top of you and / you're on the ground / kicking furiously / with all the might in your body / and you're on the floor of your bedroom / it's dusk and light has seeped from the window / no one else is here / except for your blankets, coiling around your torso / but you're still kicking.

TOO EARLY

it is 6 AM when your little sister stumbles into your room to find you wide awake and watching the window. *what's wrong?* you ask her. *did you have a nightmare?*

yes.

what was it about?

she rubs her eyes, shakes her head hard as if to wake herself up.

giant oven. scorpions big as houses. everybody baked alive.

you pull her in closer, let her sit beside you. *you too, huh?* the two of you watch the blood moon take over the sky like a rusty spoon, colossal and shameless.

you're not afraid anymore.

STORMS FROM JUPITER

some nights, your dreams are filled
with the mundane, the near-forgettable.
you'll check your emails. you'll walk
to class down the road shrouded by giant
palm trees. you'll buy v8 and shampoo at
the supermarket. but you find these dreams
are your least favorite, for their playful
tendency to bleed into the mornings after.
you are looking for emails that aren't there.
you are checking your bathroom to find you're
still out of shampoo. you're not sure
what day it is anymore. what conversations
you've had and which you haven't. your father
asks you, *have you talked to your mother lately?*
and you say, *yes, of course I talked to her*
yesterday on the phone. but you think of
the conversation you had, how you told her
you felt sick, you couldn't stop spitting up
rubies and finding broken seashells in your
pockets. how she told you the last time
she went to jupiter, she bottled up its reddest
storms. she said she can't wait to give them to you
when she comes home. that can't be right.
you take it back. you haven't spoken to
your mother in months. tonight, you dream
you're in your childhood room again, under
the dim glow of its only working light bulb.
not a single dust particle is out of place, and
you're on the phone with your mother again,
but in this dream, you are

screaming
endlessly
endlessly
endlessly.
no words careen out of your broken mouth
just guttural,
wounded sound.
you are ceaseless, you give
no room for her to respond,
but in this dream,
she doesn't feel the need to.

in this dream,
she understands.

TINNITUS

a beach in san diego. you're squinting against glaring bright clouds swirling together like frizzy hair in the sky. your little sister and unborn baby brother are chasing each other, melted strawberry popsicle dripping from their lips. your great-grandmother is building sand castles with your mother, her heart still beating inside her chest. you've never seen your mother look so happy. dozens of aunts and uncles lounge around in the light, while the waves crash into you, singing oldies at your toes.

your father's voice grows louder until it's in your ear. *you don't want to spend your spring break just sitting around, do you?*

I think I'm dreaming, you tell him, and he laughs.

you're welcome.

no— I mean. how did we get here?

your father's smile slides off into the sand. *we drove.*

yeah but. I don't know. I don't remember getting here. how did you even get mom to come? how did you convince her to occupy the same space as us?

your father stares at her. she giggles so hard, she falls over. your baby brother disappears into the sea, and no one but you notices.

come on, your father finally says solemnly. *let's go back to the hotel.* the wind picks up as he sets out across the sand. the beach fades into sidewalks and palm trees and skyscrapers. your father is striding too swiftly for you to catch up.

dad, you call out, dodging gray-skinned tourists. *I really think I'm dreaming. this doesn't feel real.*

don't be stupid, hija. he stops walking to frown back at you. *we've been planning this trip for months. you wanted this. you were so excited on the drive here.*

you force yourself to remember as the wind begins to cut into your cheeks. *dad, there's a giraffe.* and it towers bone-thin above you, peering down at you curiously.

of course there is, he replies, walks faster now. you're struggling to keep up. the waves quit singing, start chanting now.

dad, you're trying not to yell but you can't hear yourself think. it's hard to spot him, weaving in and out of the crowd. *dad, wait.*

your mind is spinning. your father is darting across thin wooden beams on all fours. *this isn't real. this isn't real,* you begin muttering to yourself as you tiptoe after him. you can't see the ground below you, or the end in front of you. everything is several miles too far away.

your feet stumble and you're fighting to regain balance. your father finally turns but his face is gone. you slip, grasp at empty air, tumble through nothing.

the wind is screeching. the ocean is shouting in a thousand ungodly voices. *this isn't real. this isn't real. this isn't real.* you're at the beach again, your sister's braids lying half-buried in the sand. your mother is frantically digging, wailing. *this isn't real. this isn't real.* the giraffe is strewn on the shoreline, tourists picking at its flesh with bare hands. it looks up at you bleakly, tries to speak before its tongue is ripped out. *THIS ISN'T REAL. THIS ISN'T REAL.*

and someone is wrapping you tight in their arms. you pull away screaming, turn to face them. it is someone you once loved. you can't remember the last time you've seen them. you can't remember the last time you hoped you'd ever see them again. but the wind has stopped. the sea has fallen silent. they reach out to touch your face and you can feel it in every nerve ending, every electrified cell.

they're so close, their face inches away. they smell exactly the way you remember. like clean linen sheets and red velvet cake and your heart shattering in your hands. you're afraid to breathe, but you want to cry.

you're not real, you finally say weakly.

an emotion you can't decipher flickers across their face. they open their mouth, eyes glowing blinding white, and an ear-shattering train whistle billows out.

MOON WORSHIP

you're on a soccer team with all the girls who ever bullied you. you haven't played soccer since you were seven years old and show up late to the match wearing only half your uniform, your jersey tucked into a denim skirt, your sneakers covered in flowers. the team makes you stand on the sidelines even though they're one woman short. when the other team scores, the girls say, *that's not fair. the sun's in our eyes. we can't see shit.* so the sun takes one look at them and implodes, crumbling into herself like a ball of paper. your ears ring with her dead howls, it's raining ashes. in the sun's place rises the moon, yellow and pitted, her enormous face trembling with fury. but you've learned your lesson by now. you fall to your knees and flatten yourself to the earth. *look at her,* the girls say, *fucking worshipping the moon. what a—* and their bodies drop like burning flower petals. you let out the breath you didn't know you were holding, look at the scorched world around you. you still have all your fingers. all your teeth. and for the first time, the moon is smiling.

ACKNOWLEDGMENTS

The title, *Day Residue,* refers to day's residue, the concept from Sigmund Freud's psychoanalytic theory.

The title of the piece "Guillotine of Sunlight" is from *Guillotine of Sunlight, Guillotine of Shade,* an art installation made by Peter Wegner in 2008, formerly on display at the Phoenix Art Museum.

Thank you to the kind editors of the following journals, where my poems first appeared, often in earlier versions:

"Garden Lungs," "Guillotine of Sunlight" (formerly titled "Pieces of a Dream You Can't Remember"), and "*Drive Drive Drive*" : *Pussy Magic.*

"Tooth Decay" and "Storms from Jupiter" : *Moonchild Magazine.*

"Bath of Tears" : *Mojave He[art] Review.*

"Recurring Nightmares" : *Wrongdoing Magazine*

Wanda Deglane is a poet and therapist from Arizona. She is the author of *Melancholia* (Vegetarian Alcoholic Press, 2021) and other chapbooks.

www.ingramcontent.com/pod-product-compliance
Lightning Source LLC
LaVergne TN
LVHW020535160826
845677LV00015B/4063

* 9 7 9 8 7 1 5 0 7 1 1 3 2 *